JOHN BURNINGHAM'S

NUMBERS BOOK

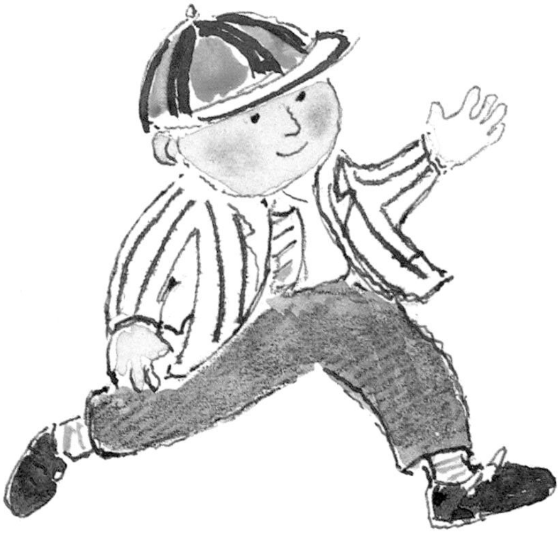

WALKER BOOKS
LONDON

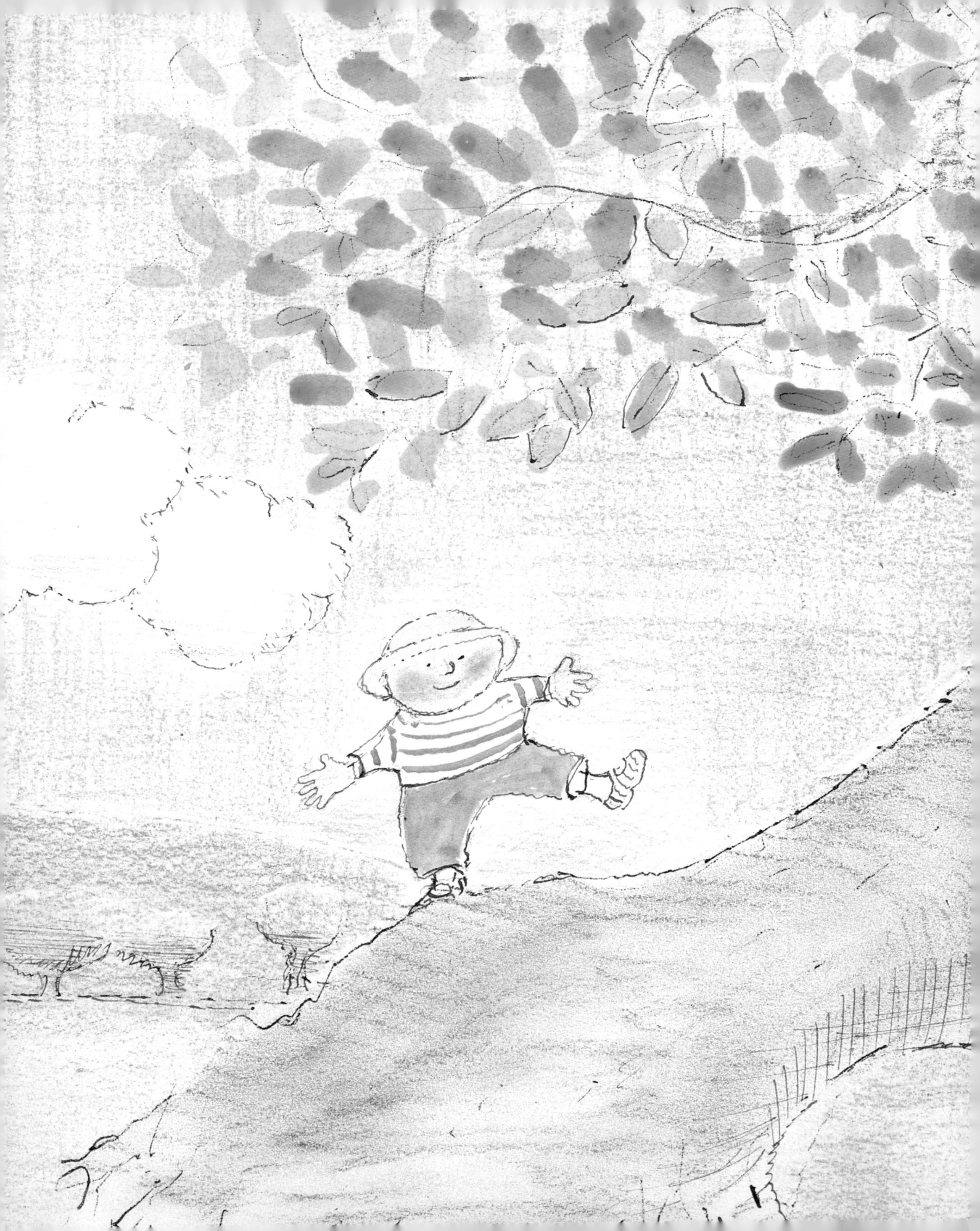

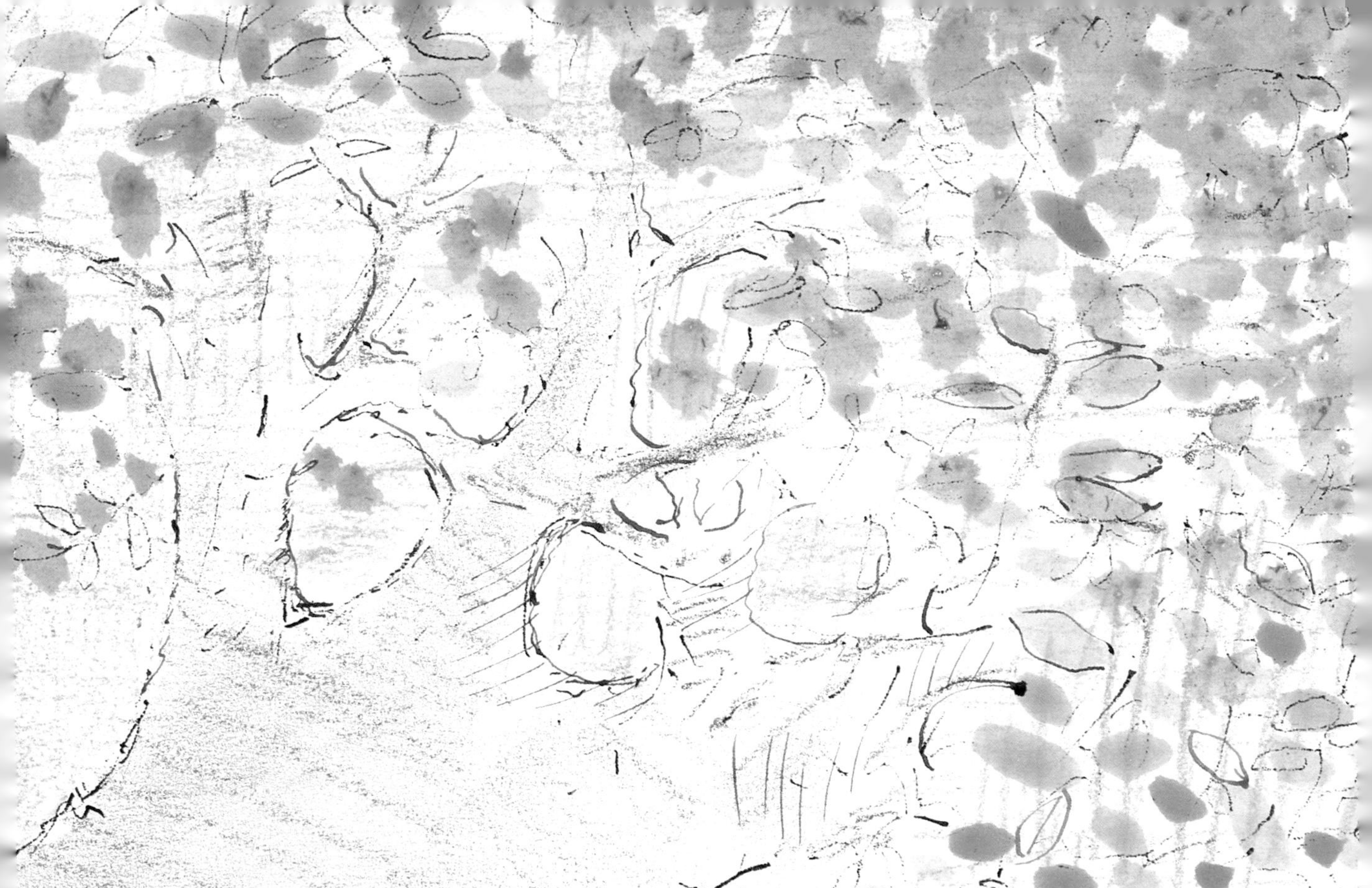

1 one

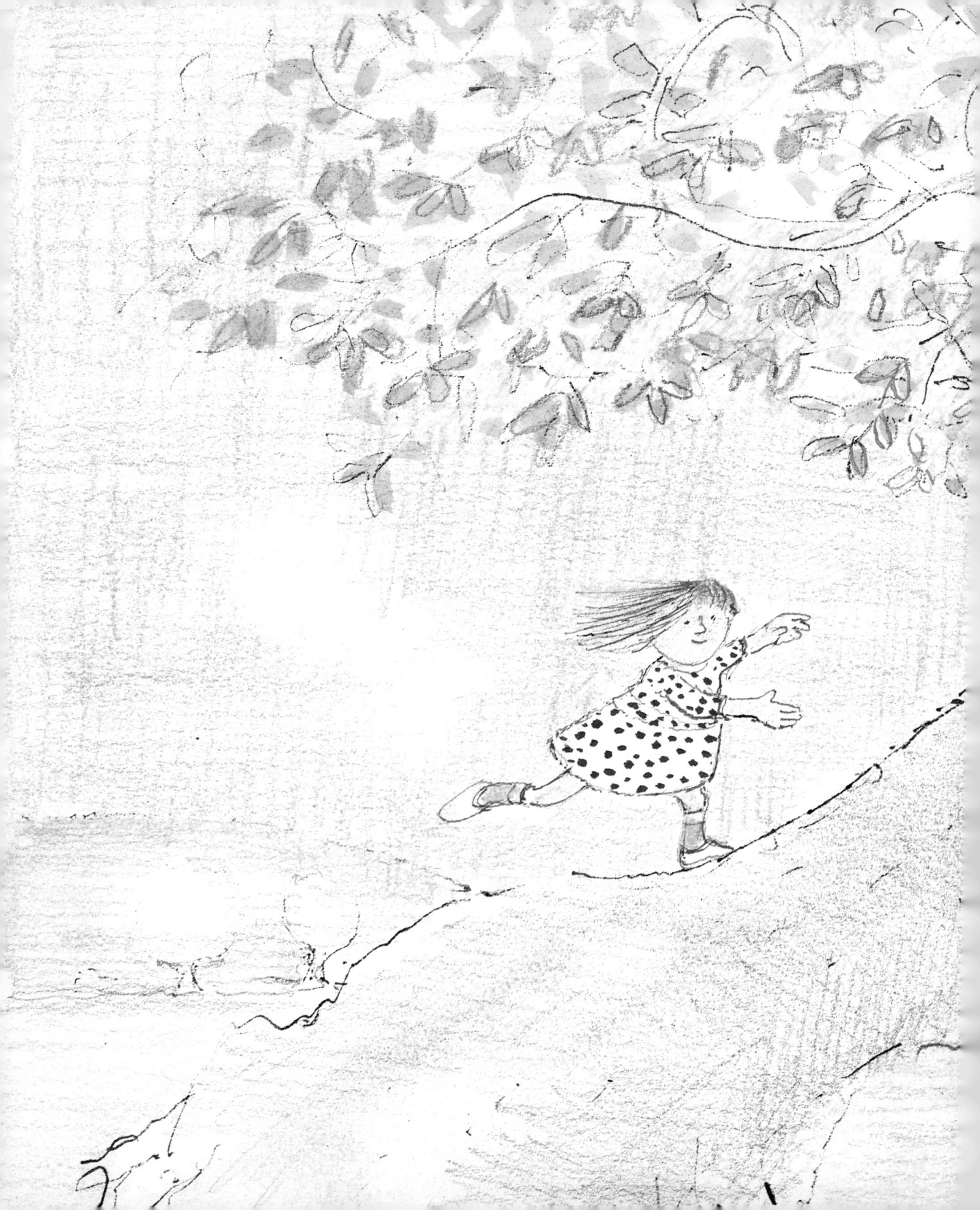

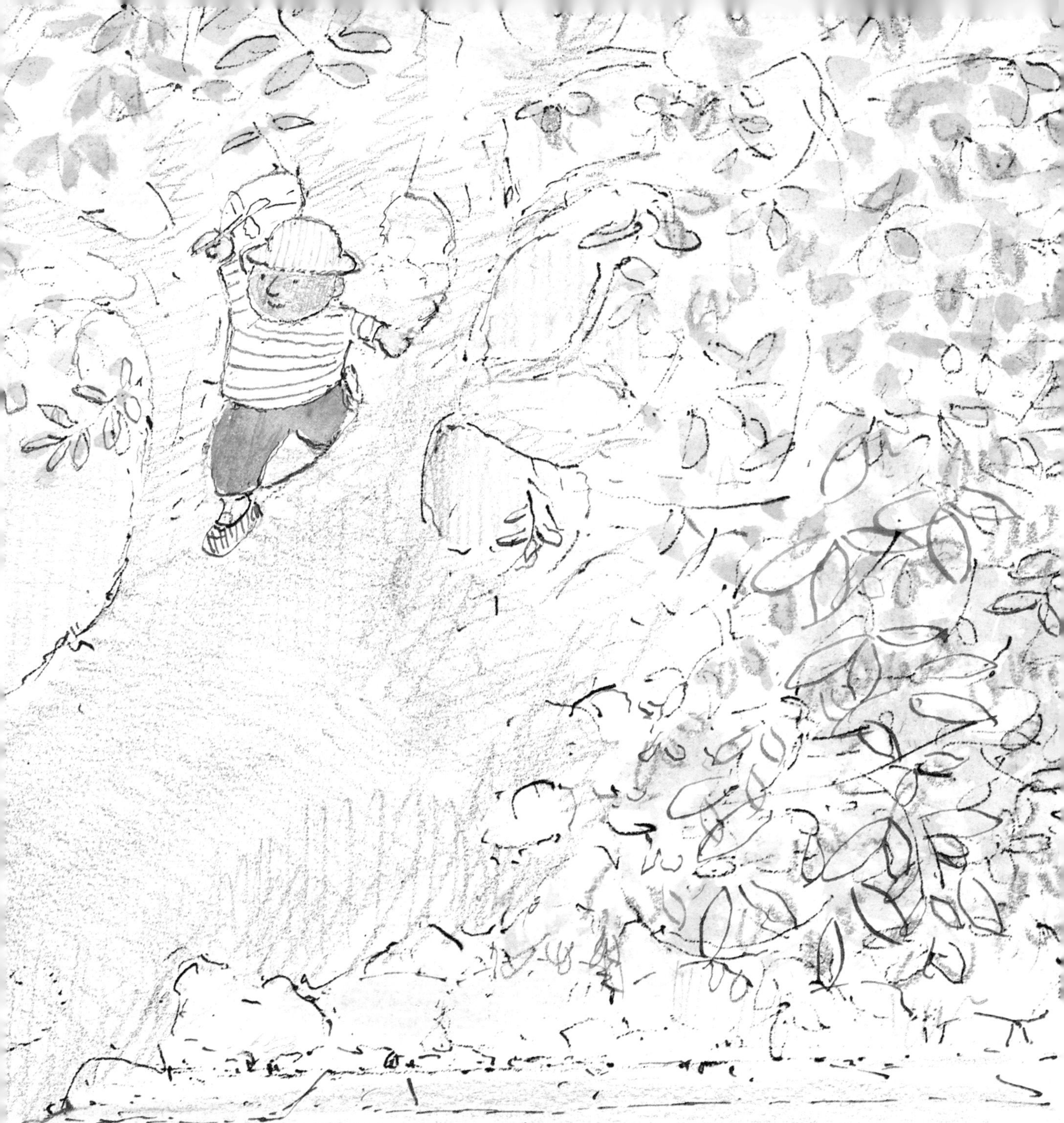

2 two

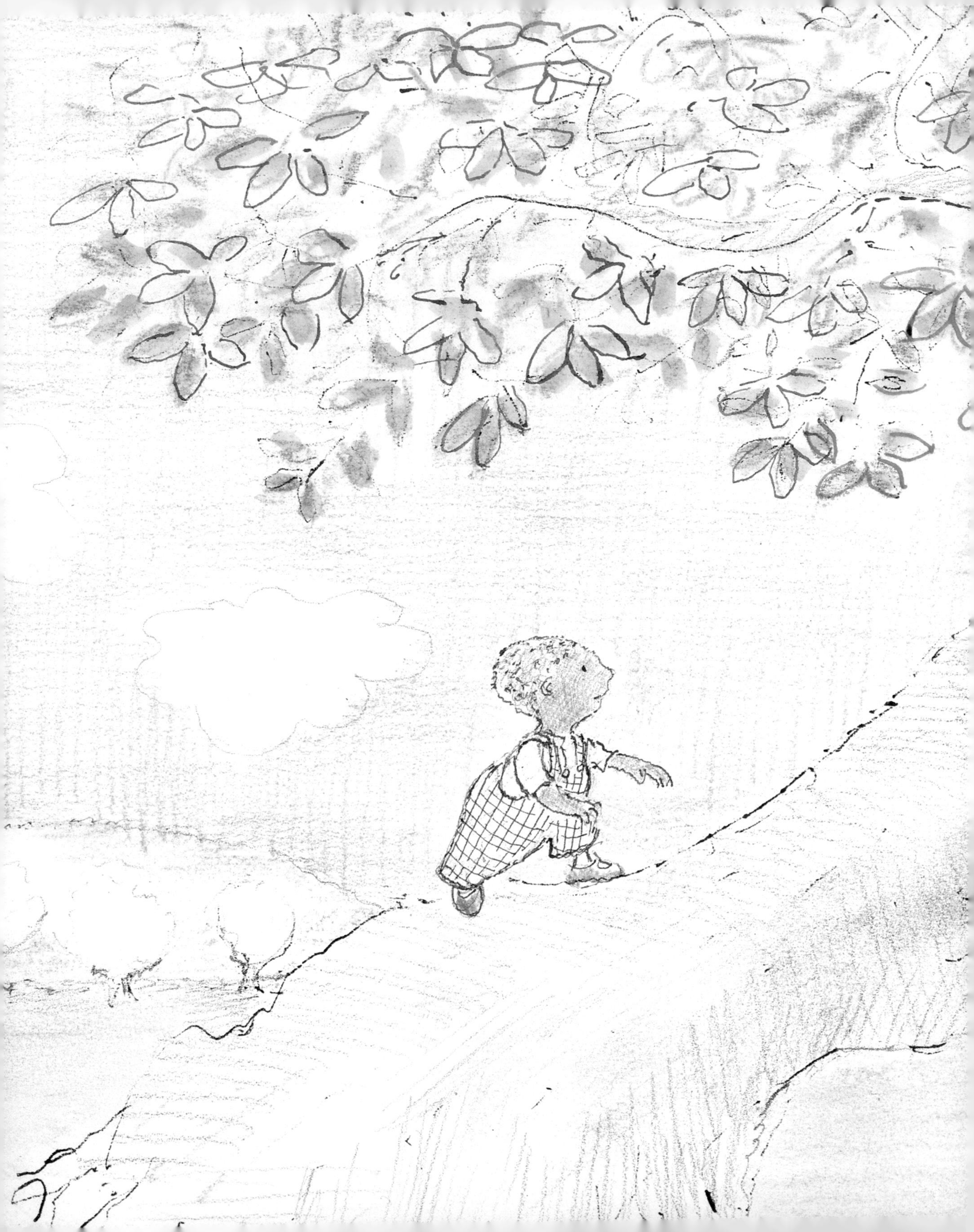

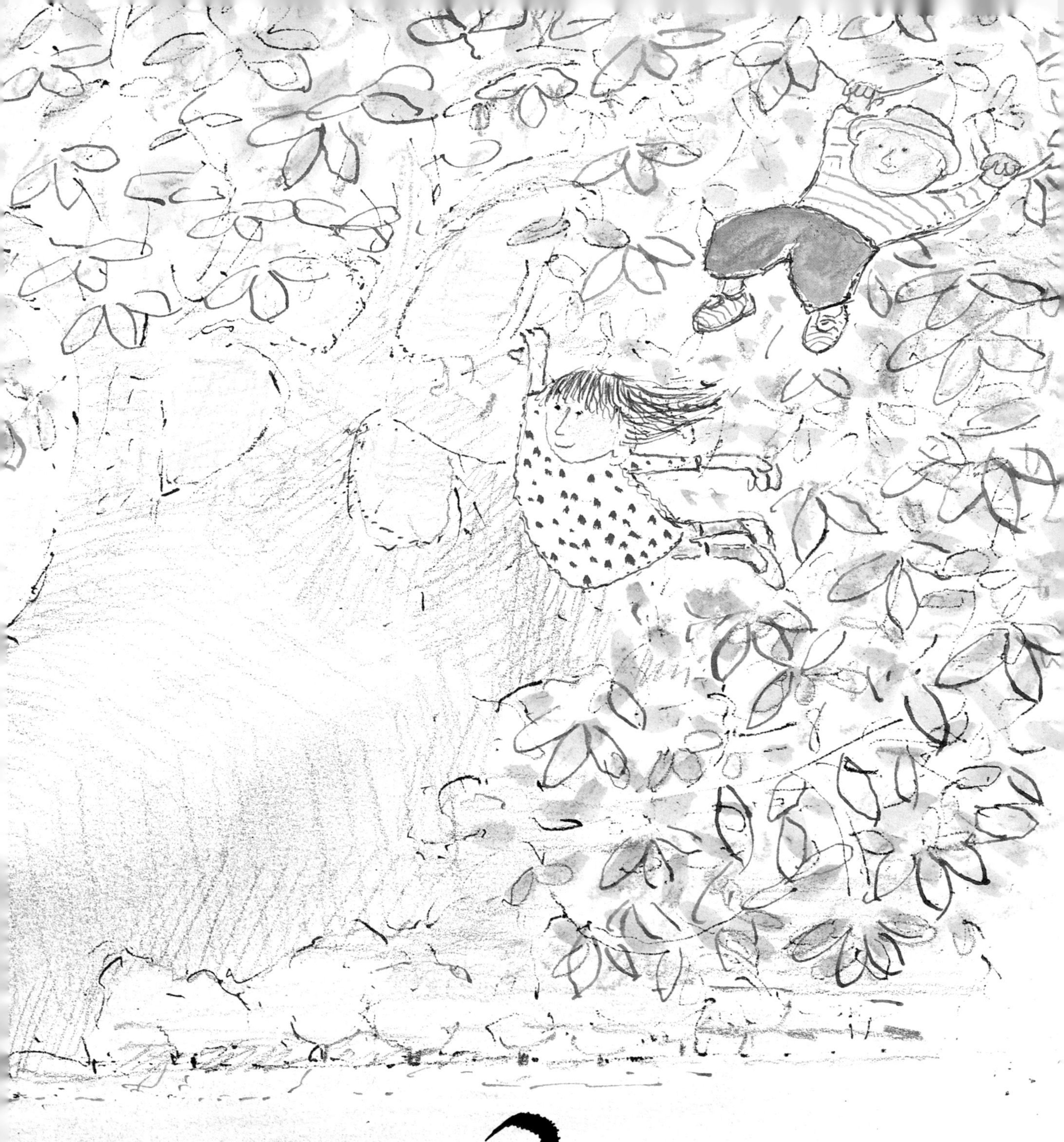

3 three

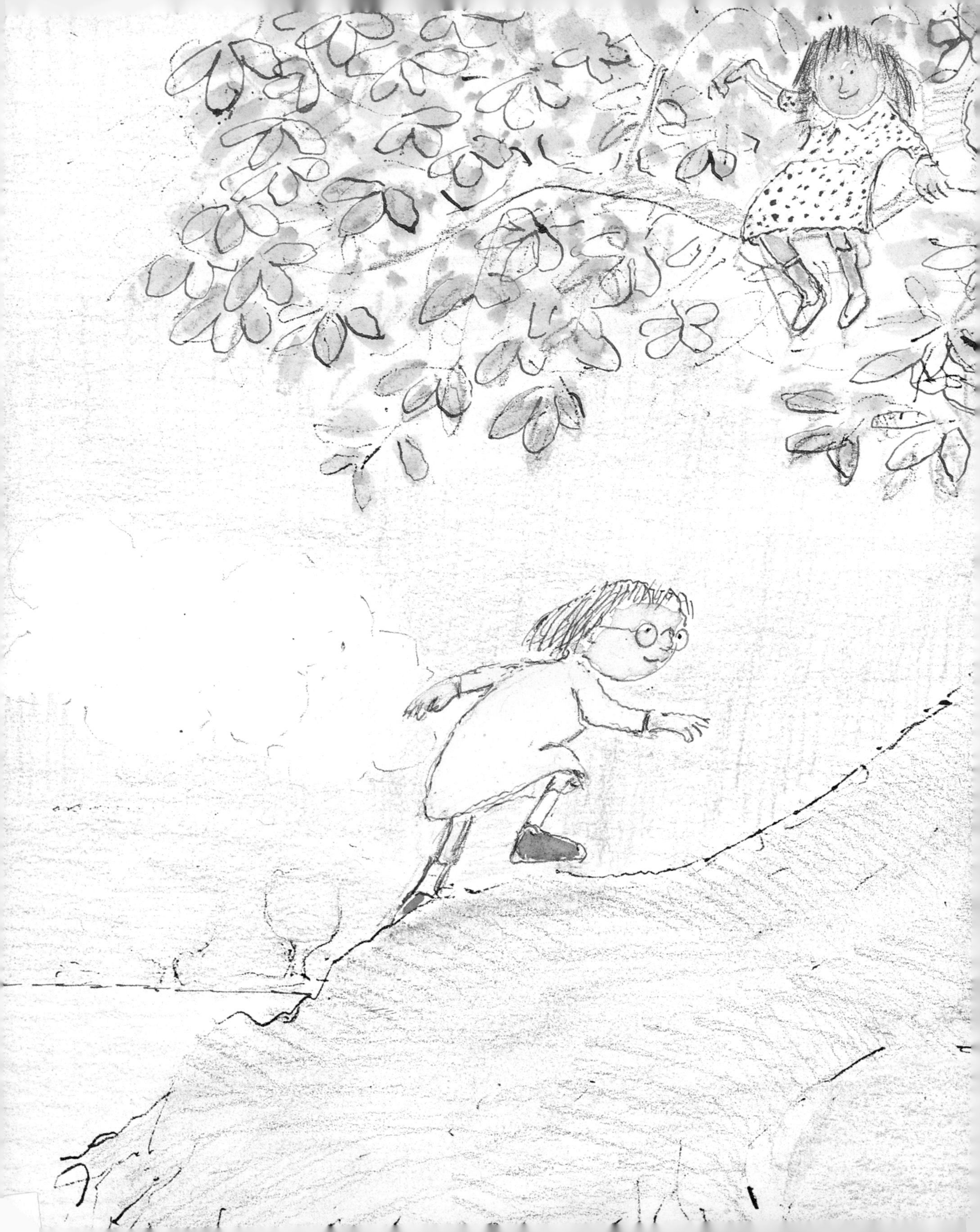

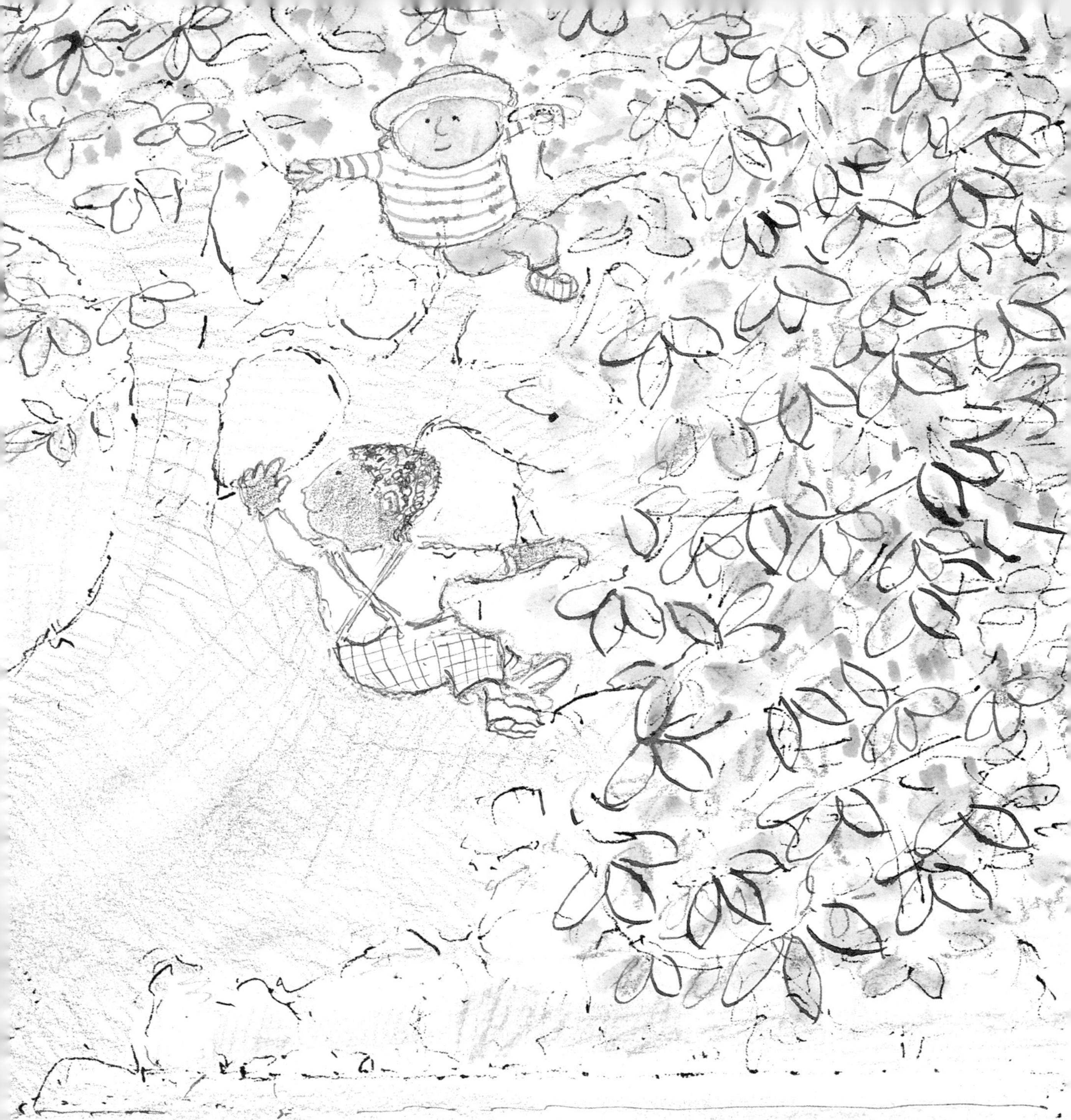

4 four

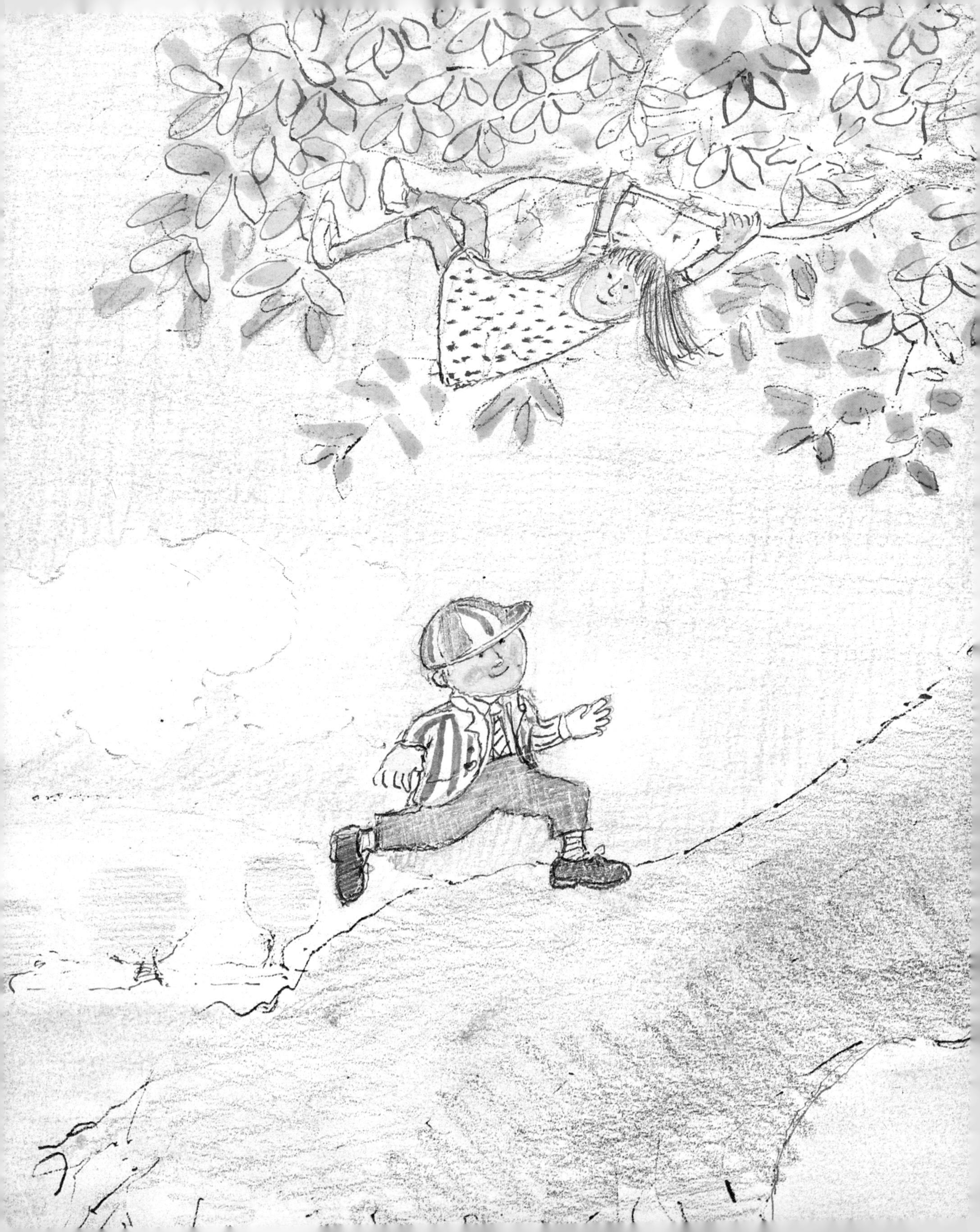

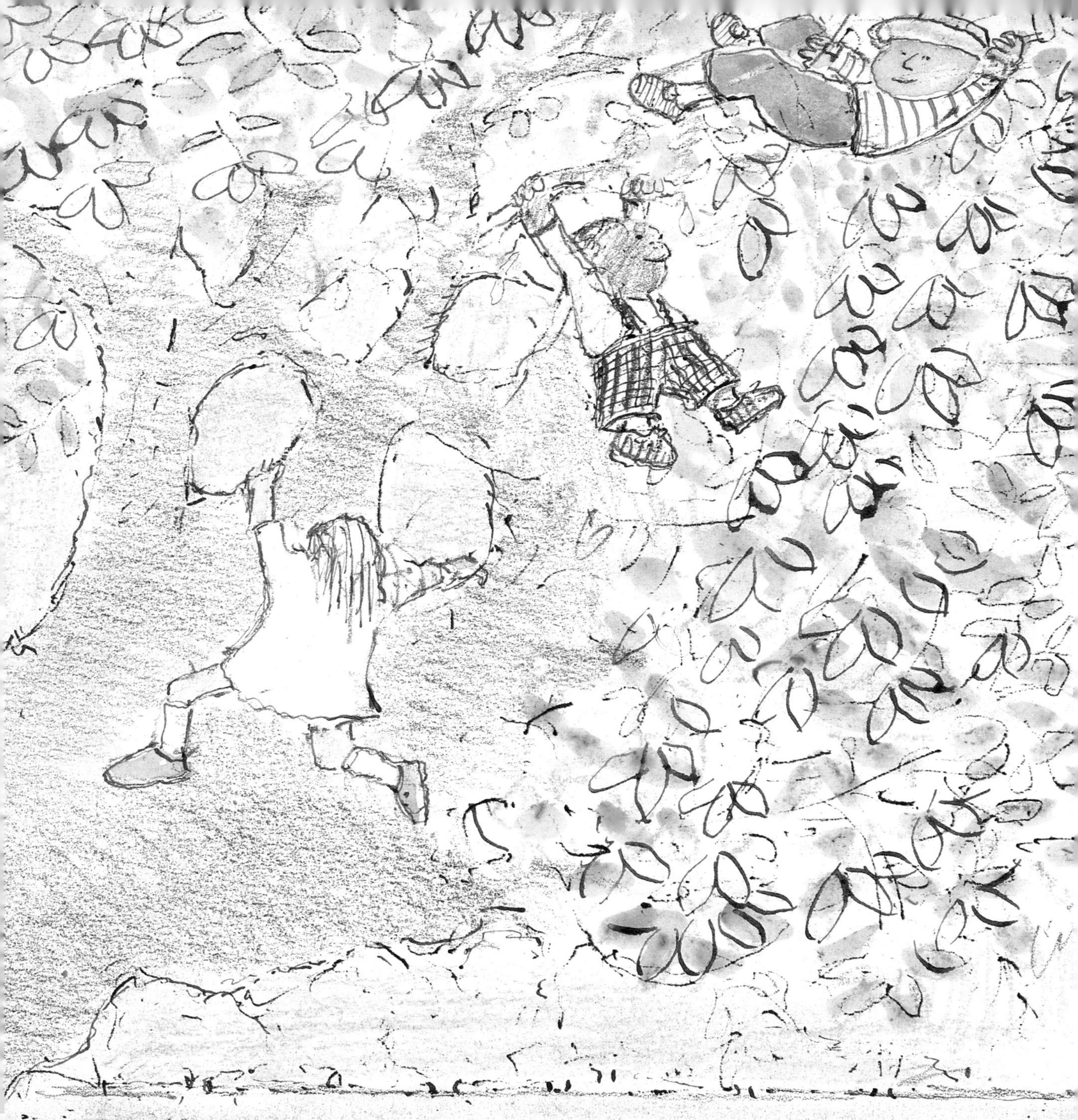

5 five

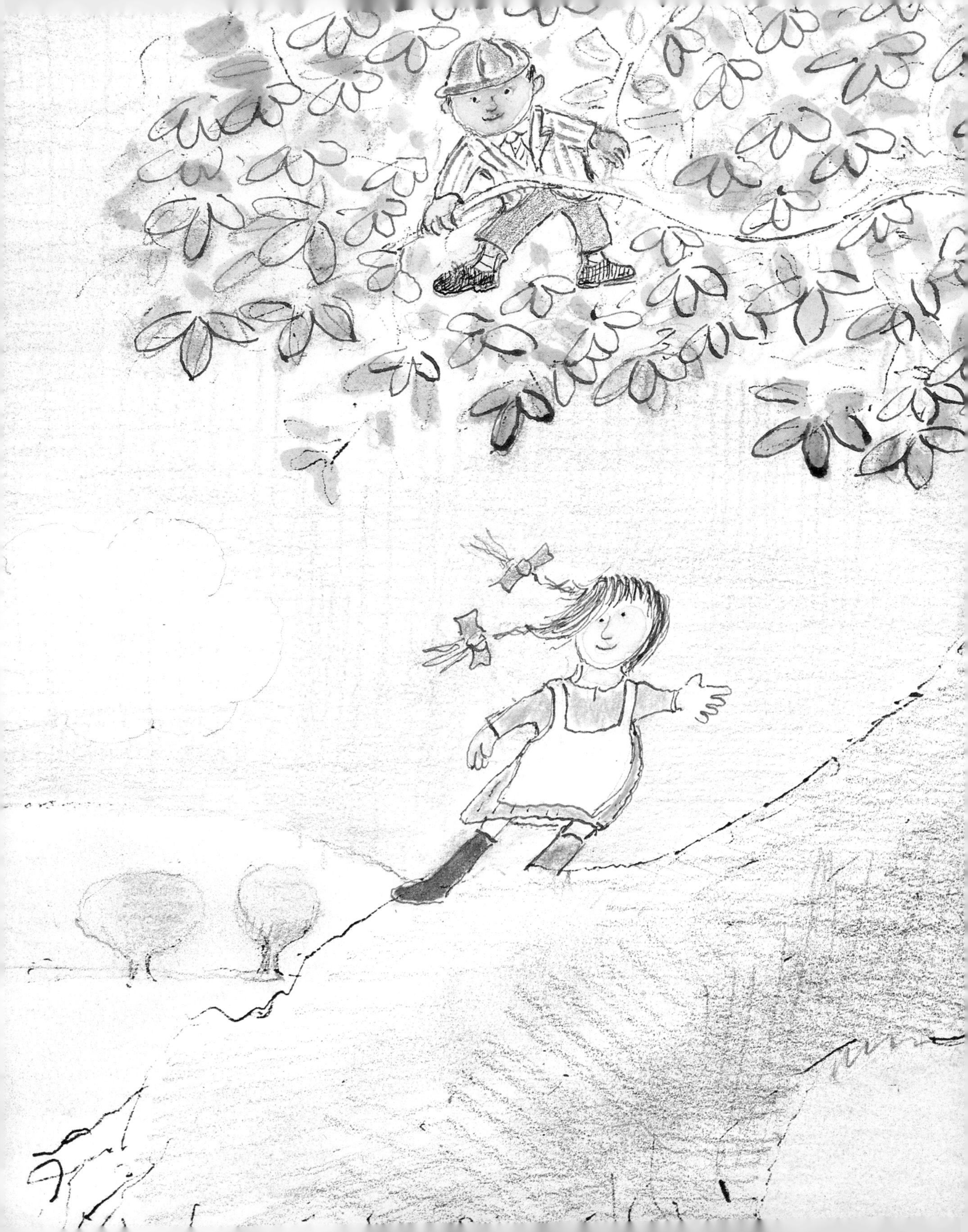

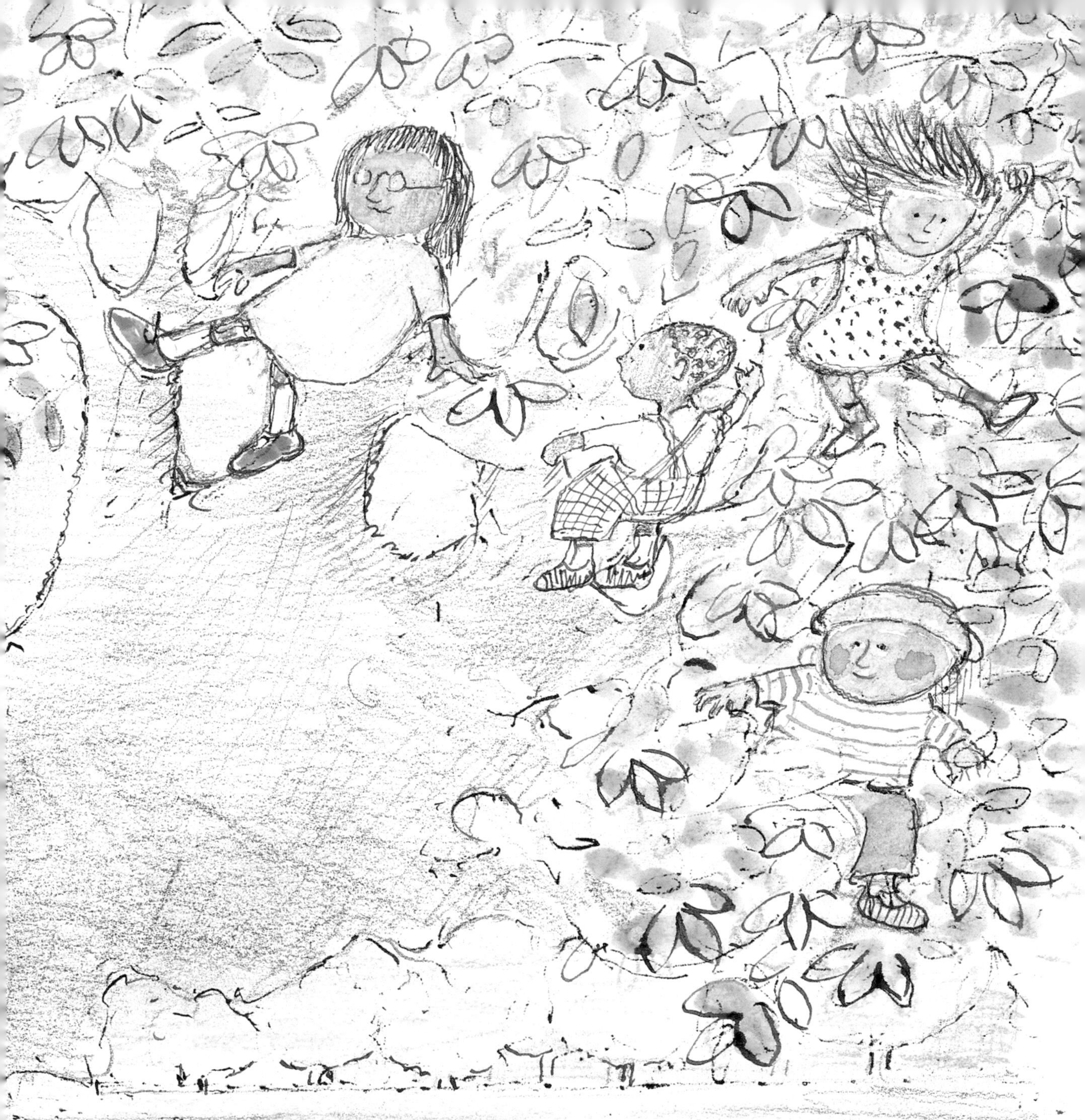

6 six

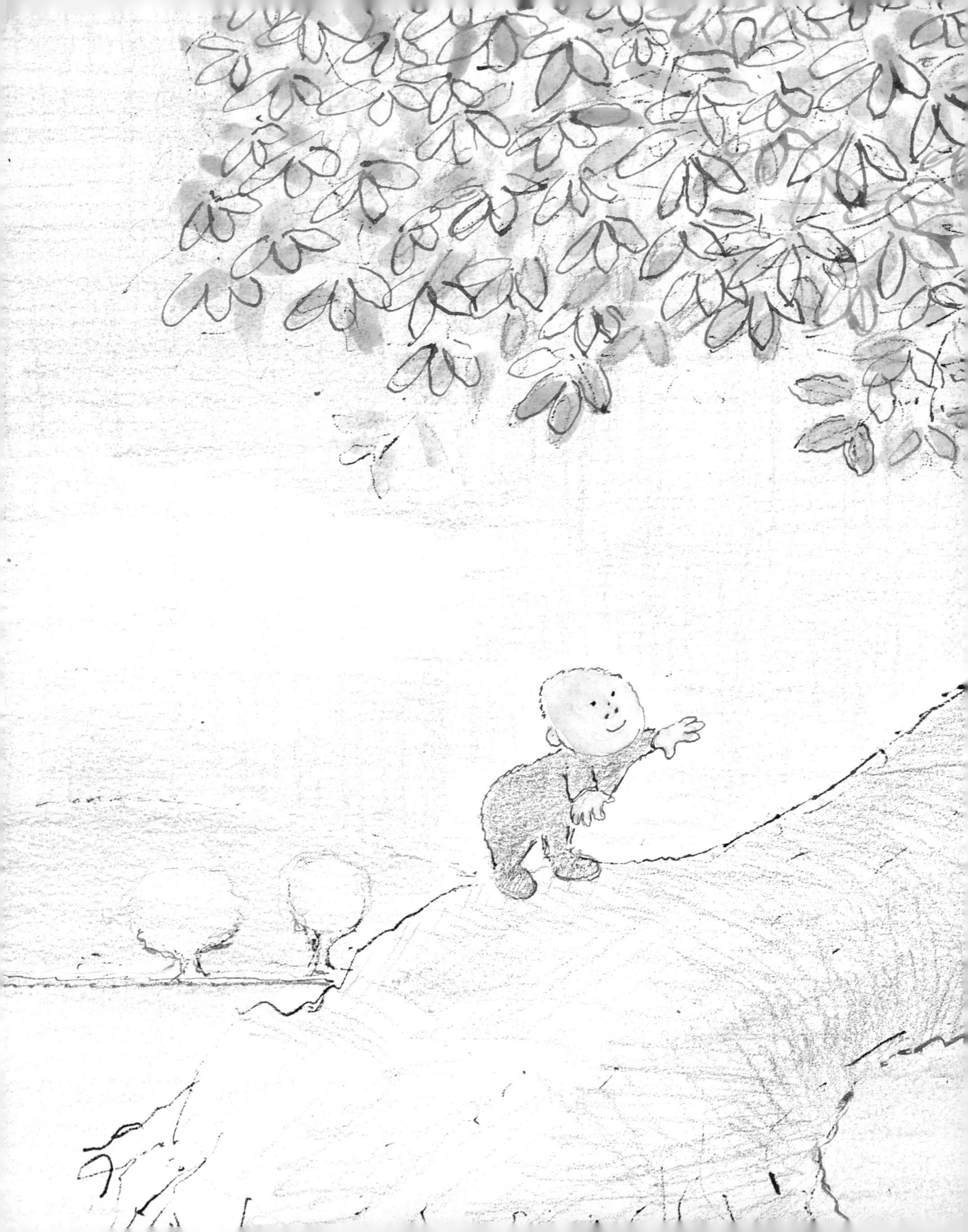

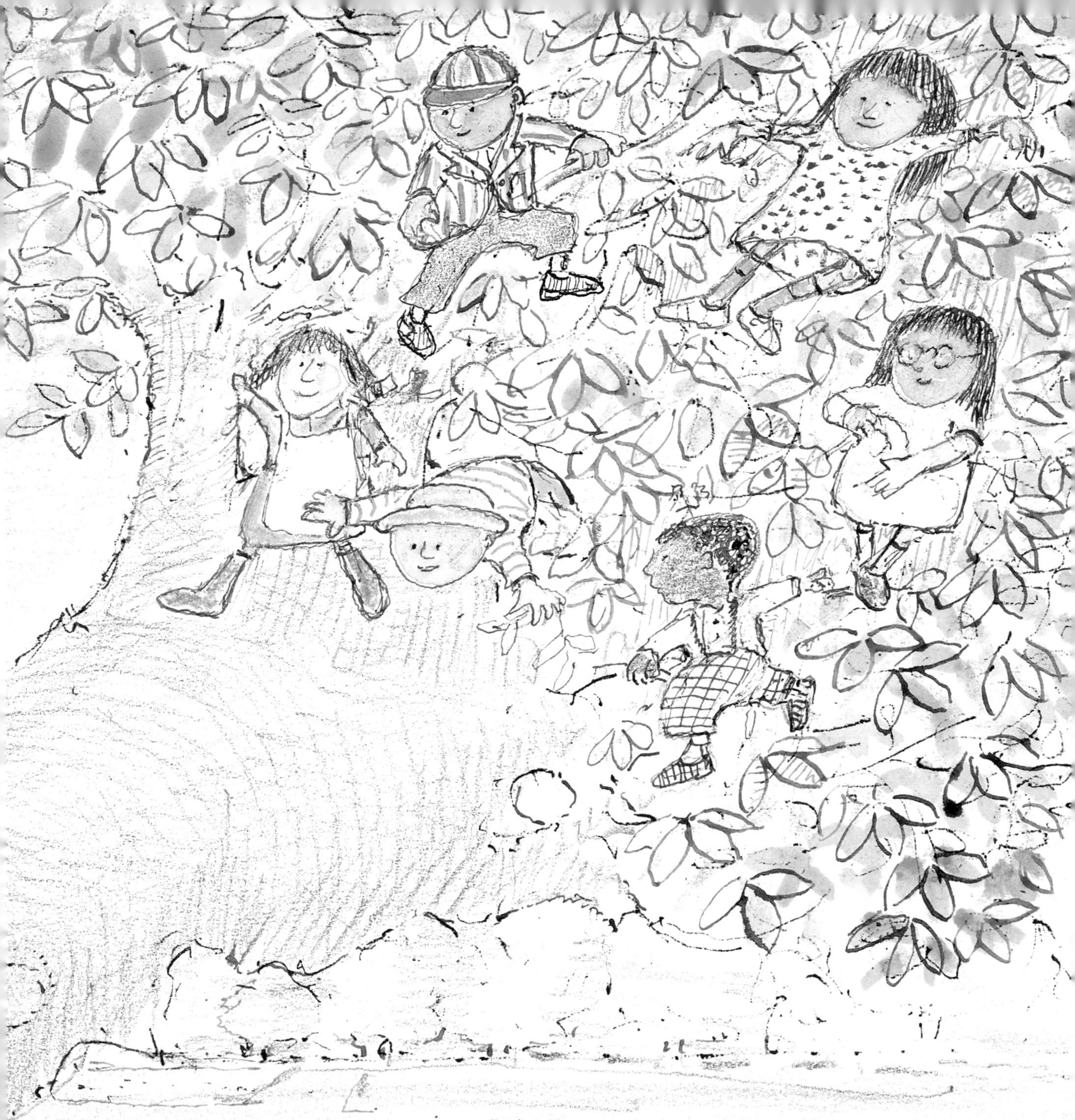

7 seven

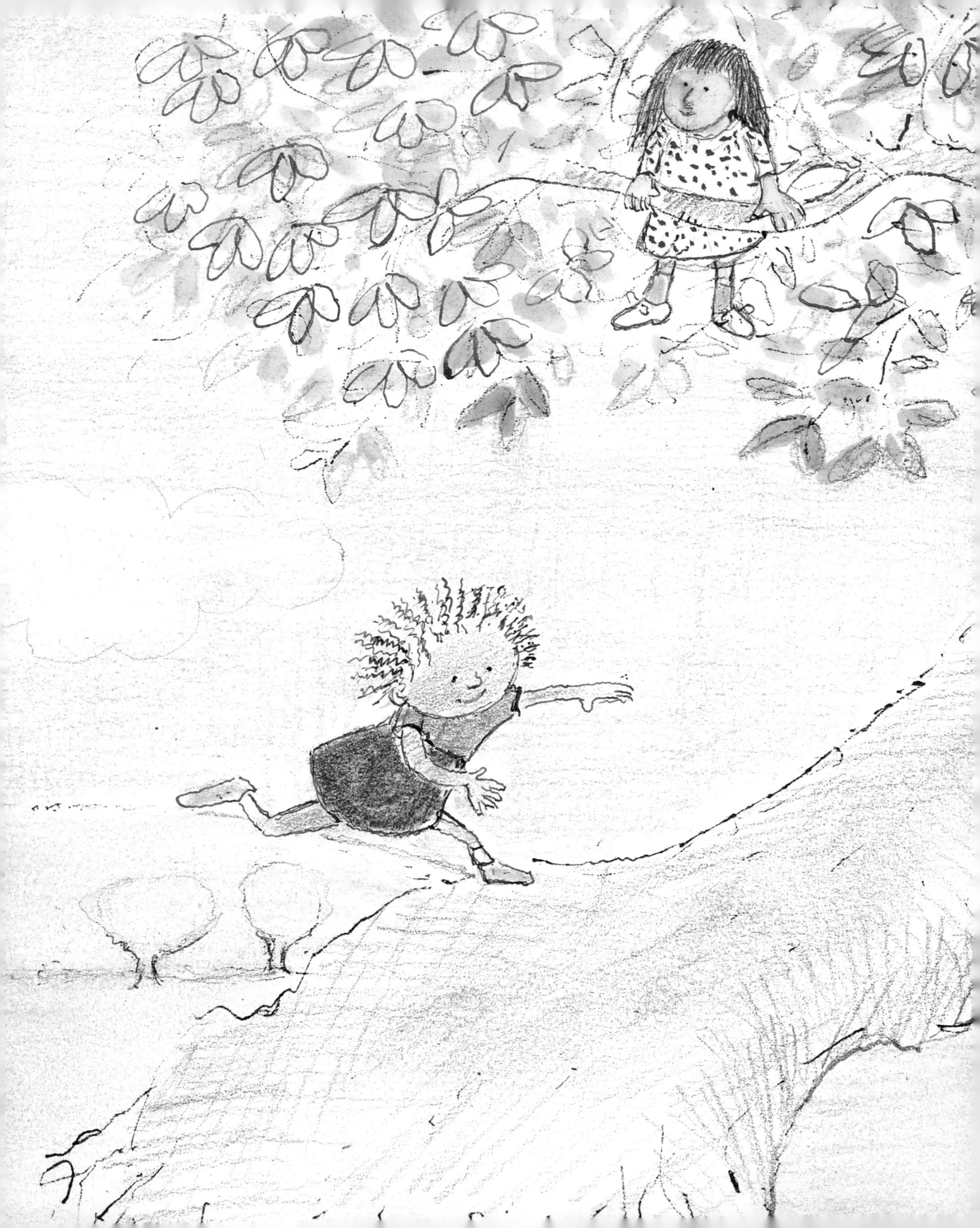

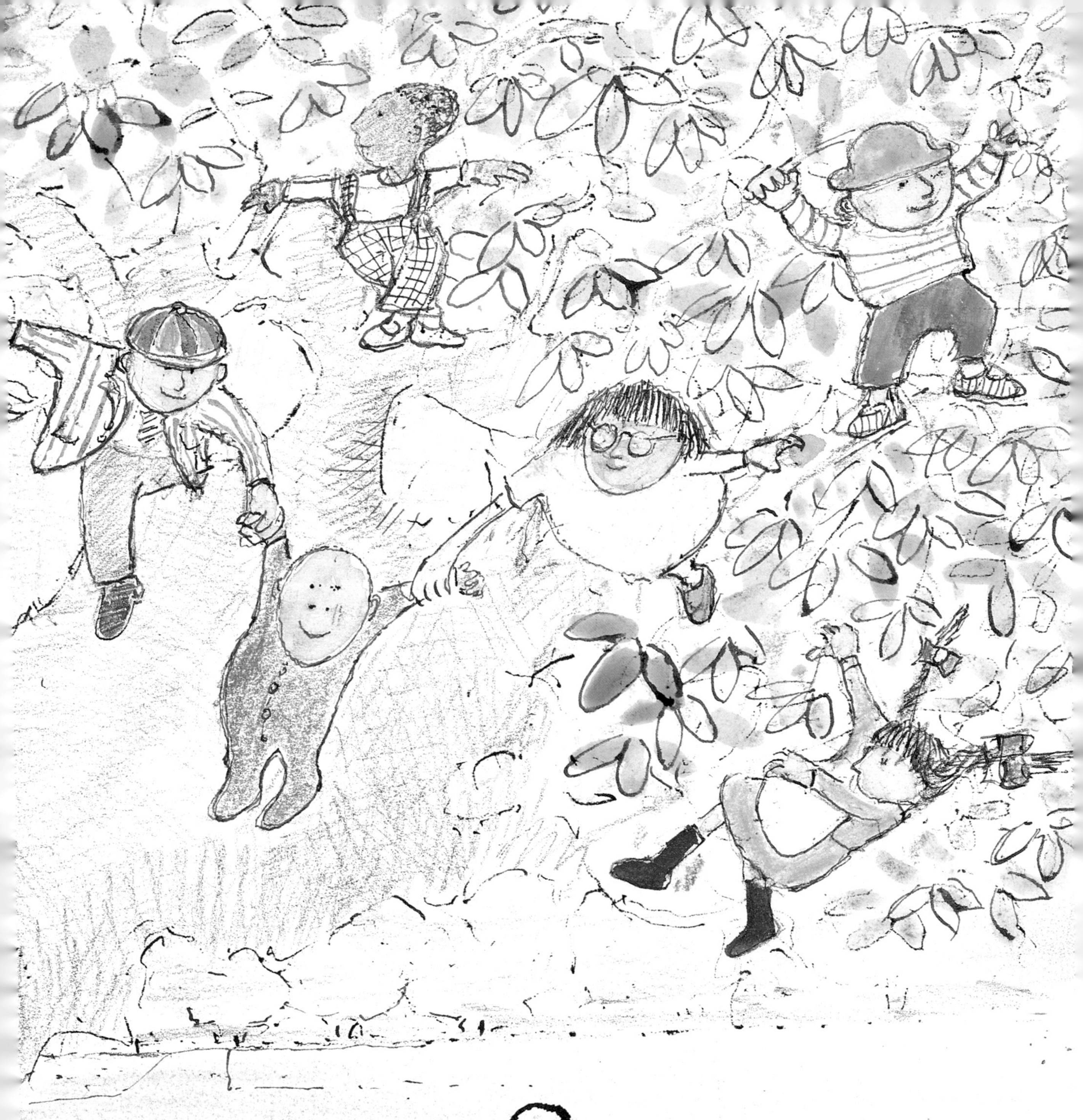

8 eight

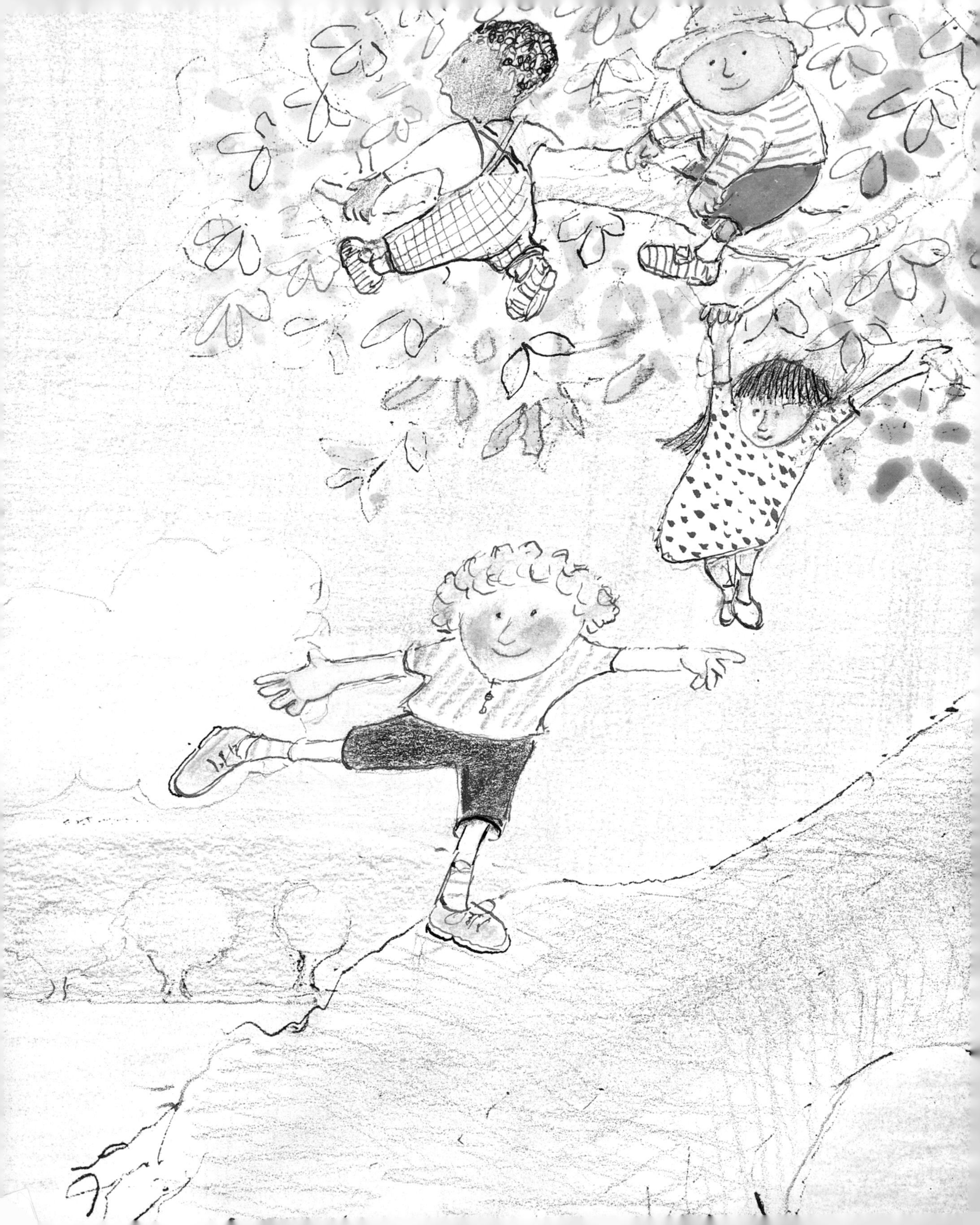

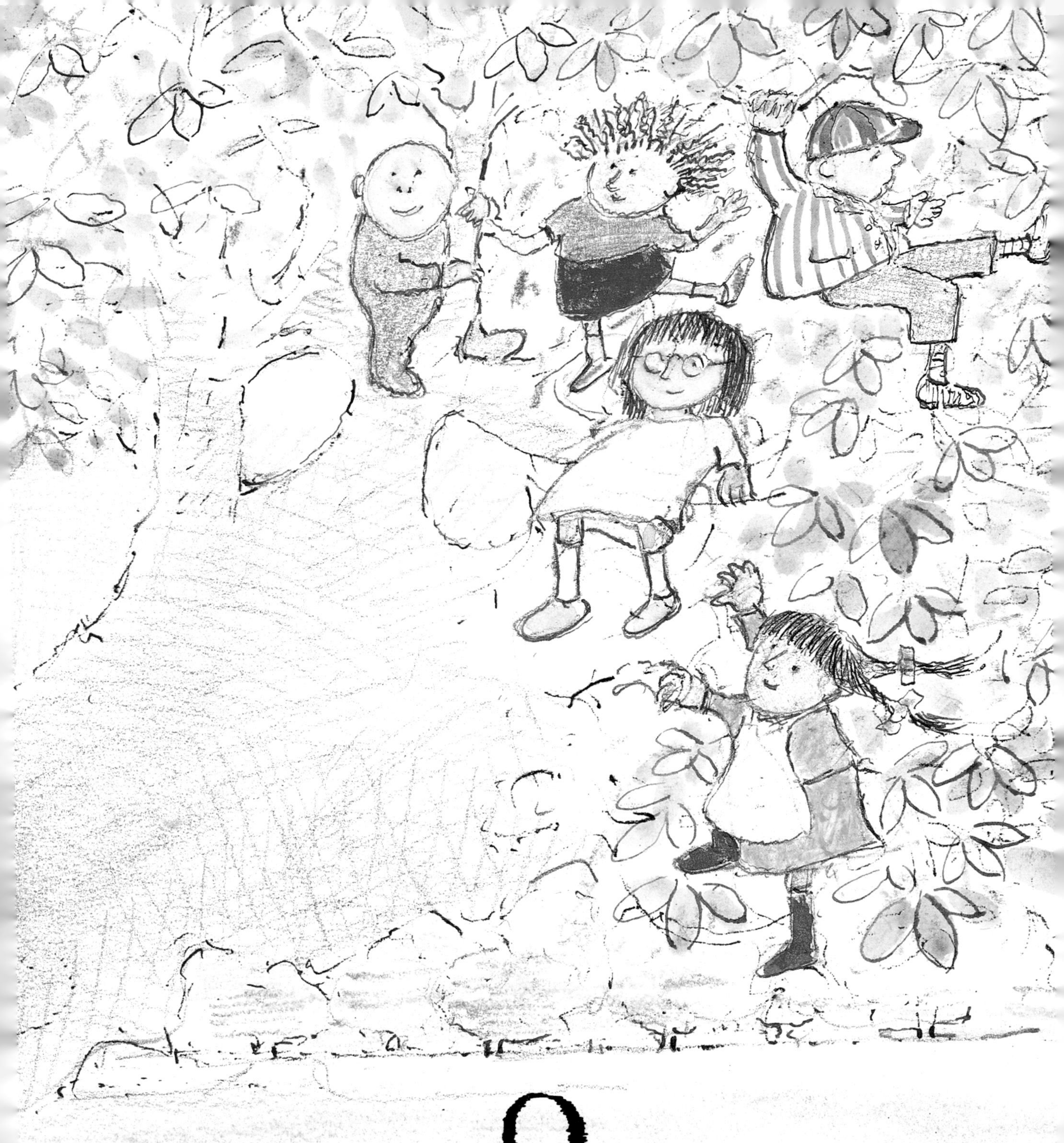

9 nine

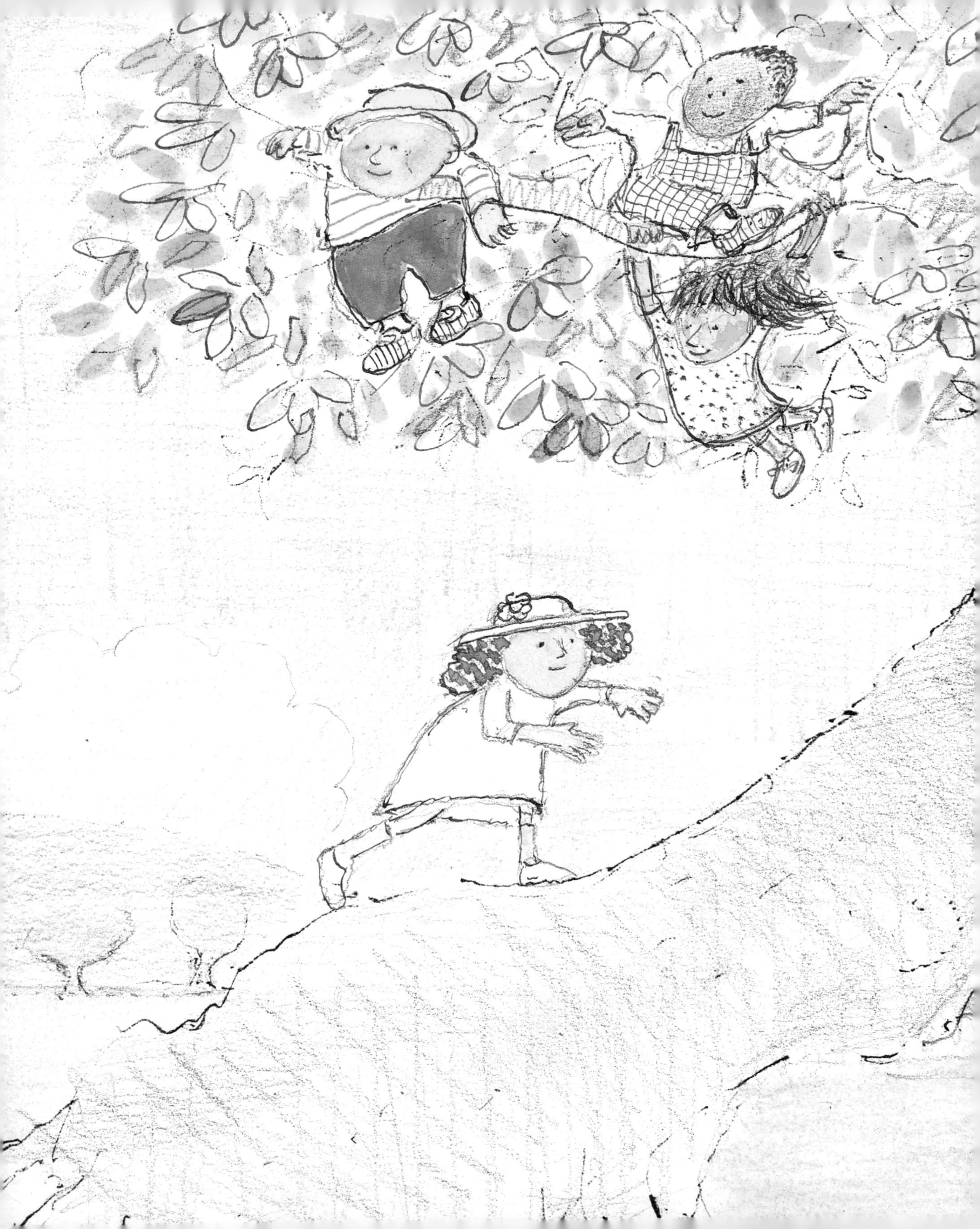

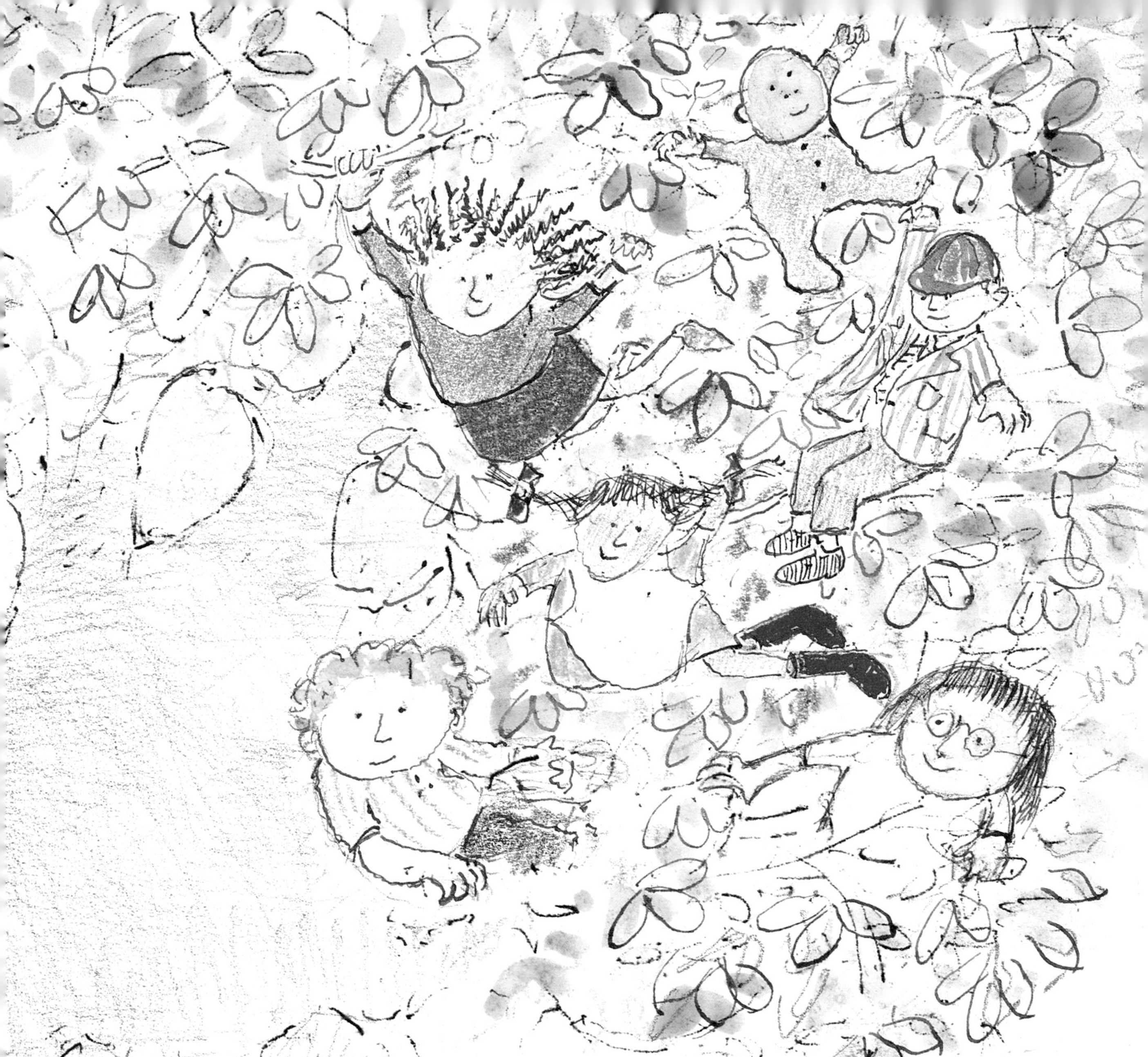

10 ten

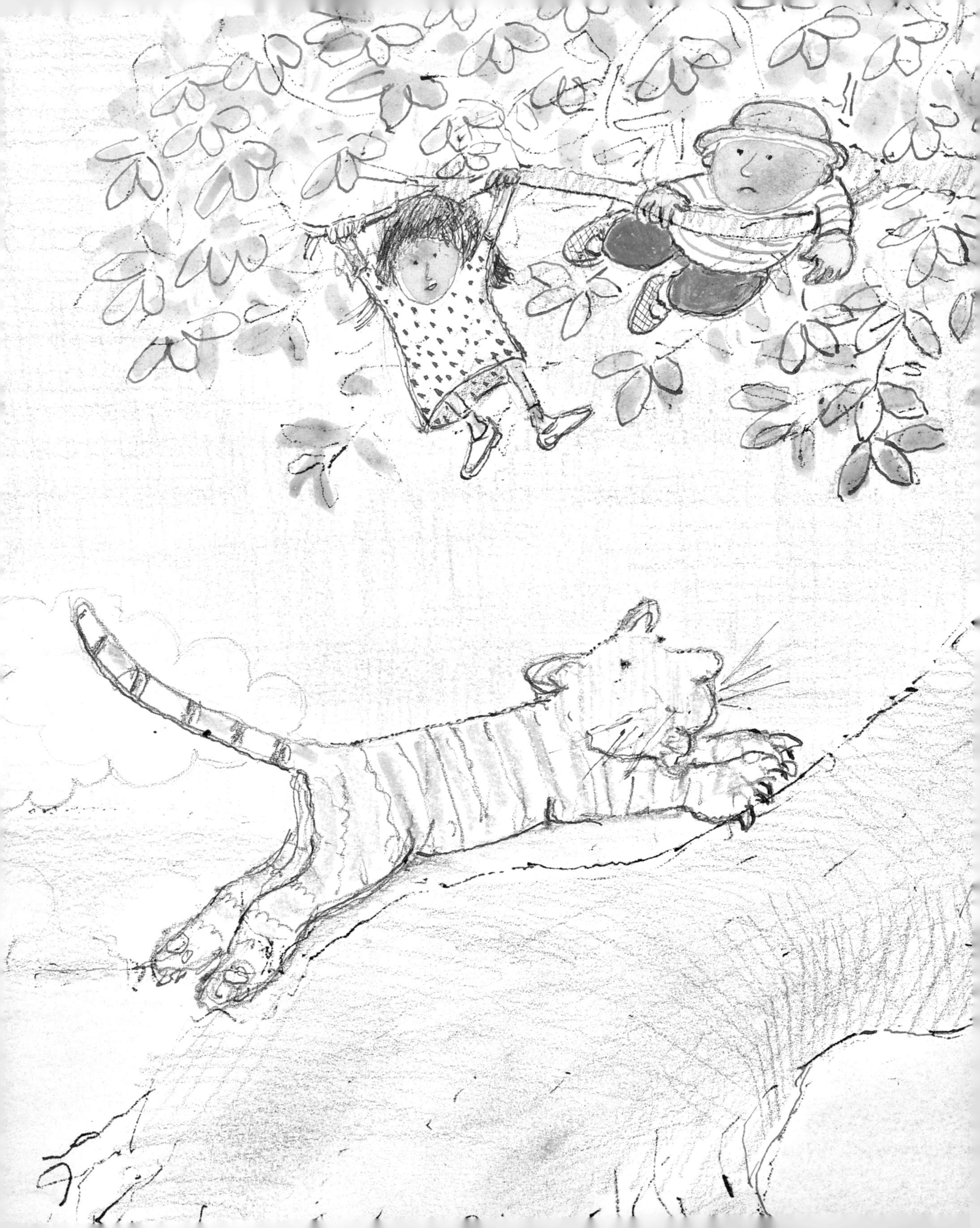

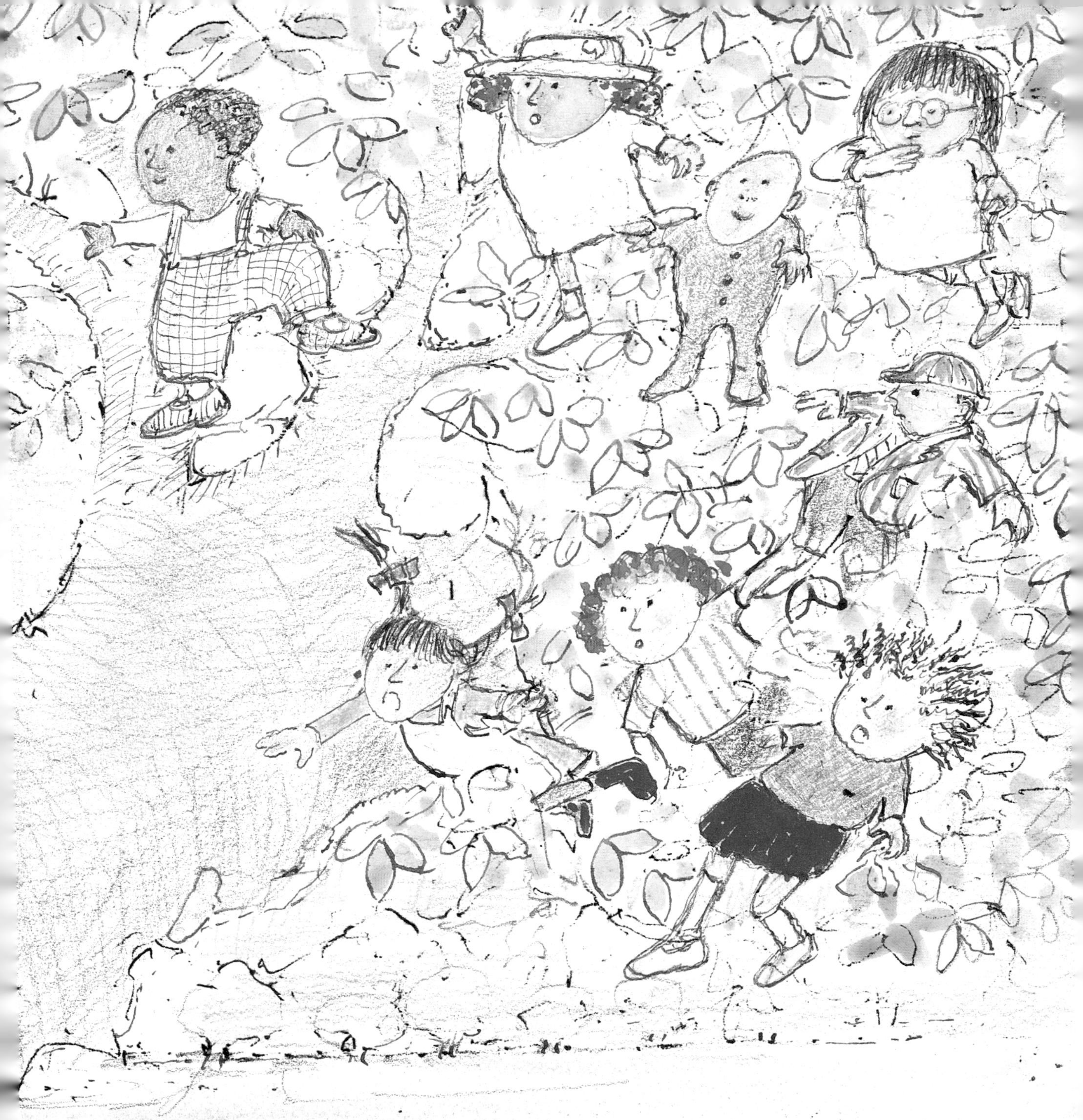

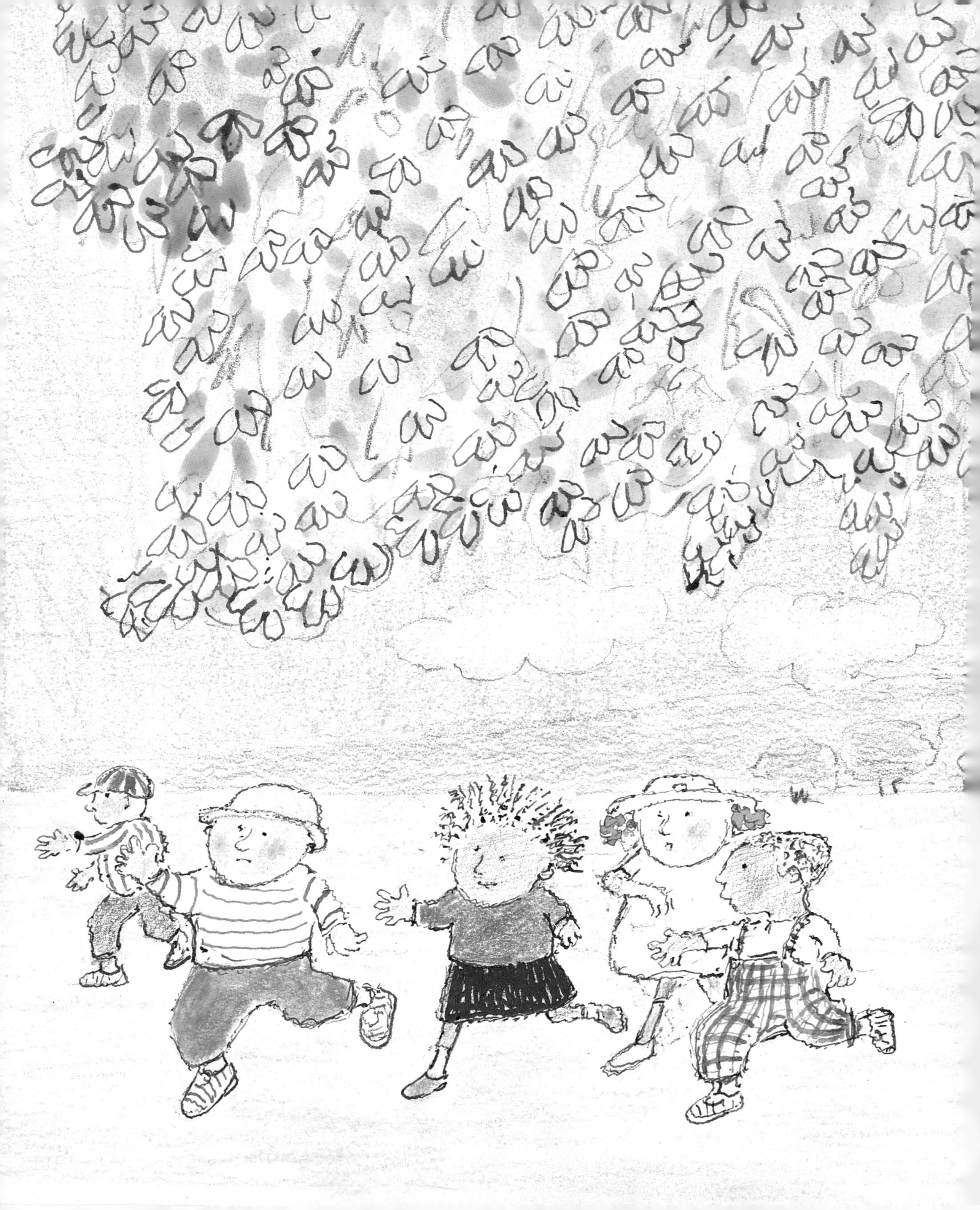

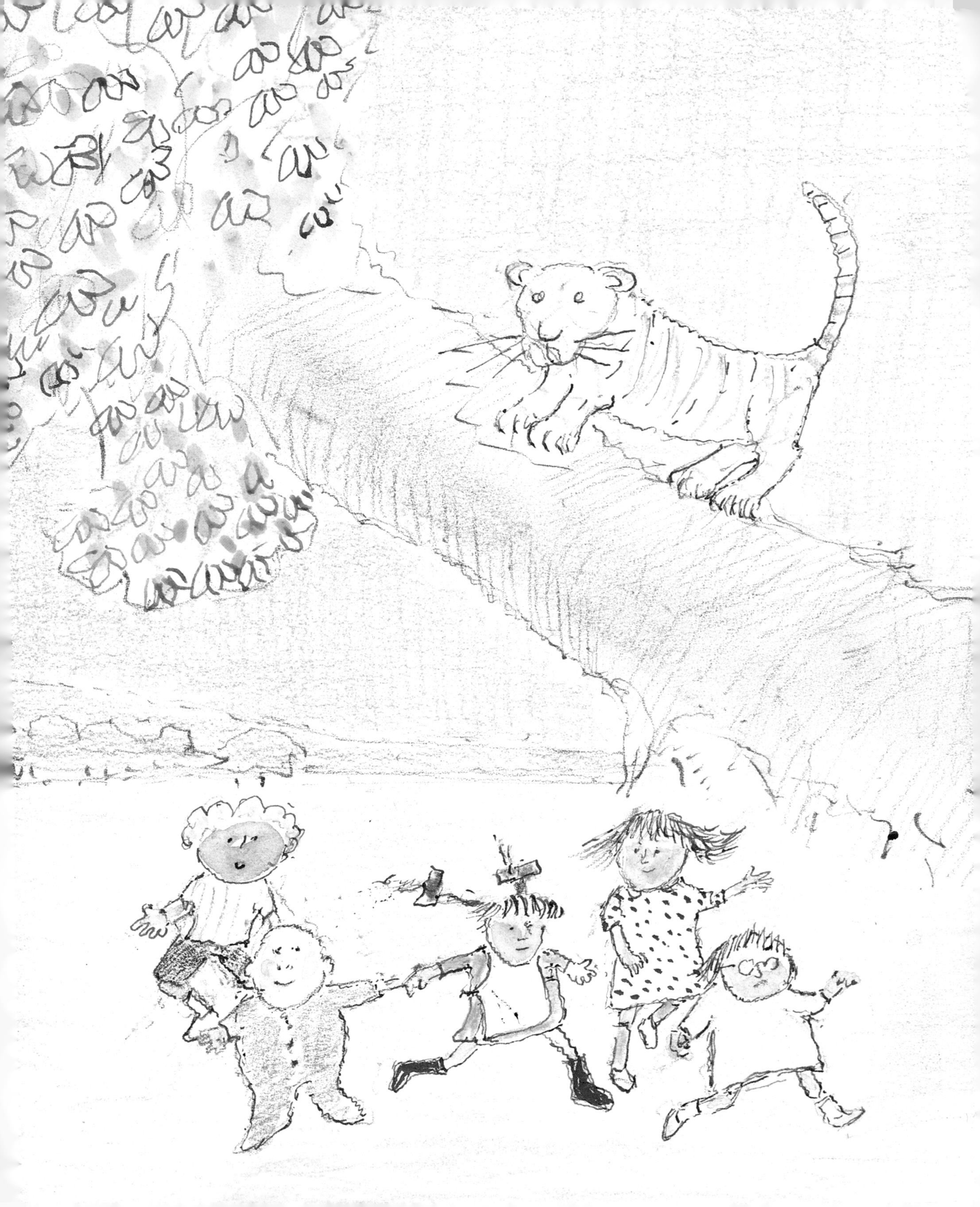

1

2 3

4 5 6

7 8 9 10

10 9 8 7

6 5 4

3 2

1